Nancy

You're just so wonderful. I appreciate all that you are doing for me to process more of the past. I thank you so much.

Lisa Sayford
"2010"

:)

OUT OF DARKNESS INTO LIGHT

Lisa A Sanford

authorHOUSE®

AuthorHouse™
1663 Liberty Drive, Suite 200
Bloomington, IN 47403
www.authorhouse.com
Phone: 1-800-839-8640

© 2007 Lisa A Sanford. All rights reserved.

No part of this book may be reproduced, stored in a retrieval system, or transmitted by any means without the written permission of the author.

First published by AuthorHouse 10/22/2007

ISBN: 978-1-4343-2226-5 (sc)

Printed in the United States of America
Bloomington, Indiana

This book is printed on acid-free paper.

Introduction

I would like to thank my children, who have supported me throughout the years during my treatment as well as their own. Their faith and unconditional love for me has kept me going. I will always love you, Tony, Devroy, Daniel, and Kara.

I would also like to thank my therapist, who if it weren't for her support and love and guidance I would still be playing the role of a victim. I love you, Anne.

To a wonderful woman who has encouraged me and has been there for me all the time, I would like to thank her. You're an Angel. I love you, Debbi.

Part 1

We go through life as a child feeling safe and secure. Things happen to us as children that we think are "normal," only to realize later in life that what we thought was normal was abuse. We didn't like it, but we thought it was supposed to be that way.

Usually some kind of trauma has to happen to us before we realize that the dreams, nightmares and flashbacks are real. They are from the past. Hi, I'm Lisa and I'm a survivor of sexual abuse and alcohol abuse. In 1998 I was diagnosis with PTSD, which is Posttraumatic Stress Disorder, and tendencies toward Obsessive Compulsive Disorder (OCD).

I grew up in a large family. There were fourteen kids. There were seven girls and seven boys. I am the ninth one from the oldest and there are five younger than me.

Growing up we used to move around a lot from one town to another or some times to different houses in the same town. The last town we moved to we ended up living in four different houses until finally we were able to afford a house big enough for all of us. Most of the houses we lived in had only two bedrooms, some had three, one even had an outhouse for us to use, so we were not rich by any means.

The big house had four bedrooms, a large living room with French doors, a large dining room and a large kitchen. I remember walking in and looking at the aluminum tile in the kitchen. I thought it was the most beautiful thing I had ever seen; it was black and white checked and boy did it shine. I thought we were moving up in the world when we moved into that house.

My father worked in a factory, while my mom stayed home to take care of the kids, until the last one went to school. Then she started working at a different factory, working swing shifts all the time.

We grew up poor. We didn't have a lot of money. Most of our clothes were hand-me-downs from older sisters or from the Salvation Army. There were times when all we had to eat for weeks was potatoes. We would fix fried potatoes with squash a lot. But during the holidays we always had our big feast.

We had a lot of good times even though we didn't have much. At Christmas time all of us would go Christmas caroling to the neighbors' houses and they would give out cookies or homemade bread to us. When we got home we would have hot cocoa and some of the cookies. One Christmas the younger kids, six of us, decided to put on a play for our older siblings who were married and their children. After the play we put my youngest sister in a big cardboard box, put candy in the box, and had our nieces and nephews open the box and then she would jump up and surprise them. So, although we had our problems, we still made the best of our life.

When we moved into the big house there were twelve kids at home, then a few years later more got married and moved out of the house. My father seemed to be drinking more and more. Every Friday we would wait for him to get home from work to give us the bag of Brach's candy that he gave us every week. That was the highlight of the week. He did it for a while, and then things seemed to change. My mom was working a lot; because it was always swing shift, we didn't see her very much. One week it would be eight to four, then four to midnight, or midnight to eight, which included weekends. I think my dad always worked the 11 pm to 7 am shift.

Friday would consist of my dad wanting his regular meal after he had been out drinking. It was always oyster soup and oyster crackers and, if it wasn't ready when he wanted to eat, all hell would break loose. We would all be scared when he got to that point because we never knew what to expect. If mom was at work on Friday nights, I would hear all about it from him. How she was a whore, she wasn't really at work and things like that. I guess he didn't like the idea of her working, but we needed the income because he would spend the majority of his money on booze. One day my mother made a spaghetti dinner and we were all sitting around the table. My one brother had his elbows on the table and my dad took the butter knife by the handle and hit his elbow with it. We weren't allowed to put our elbows on the table at meal times. But this night was one of those nights when we didn't say too much; dad was already pissed about something. Anyway, something was said because us kids jumped up fast and my dad took his plate of food and threw it on the floor, then proceeded to pick up the dining room table and throw it. He hit the glass window, putting a hole in it and leaving a big crack going up the window. My mom vowed she would never fix the window. I think it was many years later when she finally got it fixed.

My father was physically abusive, especially towards my brothers. He would go on a drunken rage and punch them, or throw things at my mother and not just small things either. One time when he came home drunk and pissed off as always, he picked up an end table. He was going to throw it at my mom. The kids had run to the stairs in the hallway and watched. I stood between my parents and told him if he was going to hit her with it, then he would have to hit me first. I was scared and didn't know what he would do to me, but I wasn't about to let him hit her with that table. Fortunately, he put the table back down and began to cry. It was only for a brief few moments that he cried. I had never seen him cry before, so I was a little surprised by him crying, but not enough to feel sorry for him. That was the first and only time I had ever stood up to him and defended my mother. My other siblings didn't say anything, and my mother sent me upstairs to bed. What happened after that I don't know. When he cried I thought it was because he was sorry, but I guess I was wrong as he continued to drink and act the same way in the years that followed.

There were times when we would see dad pull up to the house after being at the bar for hours and us kids would run up the stairs and watch through our floor register and listen to see what was going to happen. Sometimes he would yell for us kids and I would hide in my closet, especially if he started coming up the stairs. A lot of times mom was able to talk him into staying away from us and get him focused on something else. There was a time I came home from school and my dad was lying on the couch and there was a lady that I knew sitting beside him. My mom was standing there, and this woman was telling him that her son was his. Come to find out the boy wasn't my father's, as far as I know, but he could have been. My dad had numerous affairs with the women in town and none of them were worth looking at twice. One lady was caught by my oldest sister sneaking out of dad's bedroom window. Talk about dysfunctional.

When I was young I thought I was a happy child. My girlfriends and I would get together and pretend we were singers walking down the stairs and acting just like movie stars. We had fun just doing fun things. But as I got older I would stay up late and listen to music quietly in the kitchen when everyone was asleep. Most of the songs I would play were heartfelt songs like "Puppy Love" by Donnie and Marie Osmond. There was a time we had an organ where we put a disc in it and I would play and sing. It took me away from all the pain I was feeling. Yet at the same time I was expressing my feelings. I related to how I was feeling through music and I still do today. There were times I would stay up late and just clean the house because I was ashamed of how dirty it was. I didn't want my friends coming over to a dirty house. I was going through depression at that time but didn't know it. I guess nobody else did either because nothing was said or done about it.

The earliest memory I have of being sexually abused is when I was six, just before we moved into the big house. One of my oldest brother's friends came over and we were all playing hide and seek. I had hid under the back porch and my brother's friend found me. He said he wanted to hide there also, so I let him. He started putting his fingers in my vagina and having his way with me. It was easy for him to put his hands in there because all we wore were dresses; we rarely had any pants to wear. I felt uncomfortable being in this situation and I was scared. I didn't dare move. I was confused because at the same time it felt good. Later I learned in therapy that of course it's going to feel good because it's a sensitive spot. Then my mom and dad pulled up and we all came out of hiding. Another time he came over and started to play the game of carrying someone on his back and we had to pull the other team's player off the person's back they are on. Again I had on my dress and he wanted me on his back, so I did and again the same thing happened. Another time when playing hide and seek I was hiding in the woodshop that the neighbor owned behind my house and my brother that I will call James came in. He had started to put my hand down his pants, but because the pants were too tight, he unzipped his pants, pulled out his penis and had me jerk him off until he got off. I thought it was gross and the smell was bad. I didn't like it. I can still smell the semen just thinking about it. You're probably asking yourself why I didn't tell someone. To be honest, I don't know. It could be because I was scared or possibly threatened, but I really can't be sure. I was only six years old.

But most of the abuse that really sticks in my mind is when we moved into the Big House. I was seven when we moved in there. My one brother, who is older than I am, was married and had kids of his own; we will call him Mark. He would always play hide and seek with us. A few times he would find me and hide with me, I would then have to touch his penis and give him a hand job and he would touch me. It turned into a routine for him. I didn't think anything of it. I thought it was "normal", but at the same time I felt that it was wrong. There were times he would take us on a motorcycle ride and he would go in the woods and because I had to sit behind him he would unzip his pants and put my hand in his underpants and I would have to play with him again. One time he wanted to take me out to teach me how to drive. When we left, he took me on a back road, pulled over and made me give him a hand job again, and then taste the semen. It was disgusting. Talk about sick. Years later when I confronted him he said, "We were just kids." Well, no, only half of that is true because he was an adult. This went on for years. When I look back it felt like a tag team. My other brother, whom we will call James, started in the game of "Let's tag Lisa". There were numerous times when the same routine came into play, like hide and seek; we would hide in the play house we had made out of the chicken coop. Like I said, it was like routine for me, same scenario just a different brother. One incident sticks out in my mind the most: the boys had a bedroom with a walk-in closet and in the closet they had three cushions lying on the floor in a row like a bed. It was a beautiful summer day and the room was hot. James had laid me on the cushions and had raped me. I can still feel the sweat of his body on mine when I think of this moment. I didn't know it was rape. I was 13 or 14 but again I thought it was "normal". I didn't say anything to anyone because I didn't know any better. Then another brother came around, we will call him Brian. Brian knew what was going on and one night he came into my room when my sister was asleep and told me if I didn't let him touch me he was going to tell mom. Well, of course, I didn't want to get into trouble, so for years he would come into my room and put his fingers into my vagina. Every time he would come in I would just lie there and pretend I was asleep. I never knew which night he was coming in, but during these times I would pretend I wasn't there and when he left I would rock my head back and forth until I would fall asleep. Again this went on for years. We had no boundaries growing up.

Because of this sexual abuse I thought it was okay for anybody to do this to me. I used to baby-sit for a neighbor. Her husband would stay home sometimes and when I would read to his daughter sitting on the floor by the couch he would lie on the couch and put his arm down and under the book and put his hands in my pants. There was one occasion when he took a bunch of us girls out driving. I was sitting on his lap, I think it was Halloween and I don't know if he did anything to the other girls or not, but when it was my turn he would play with my vagina. They finally moved. I started babysitting for a friend of ours. Her husband had introduced me to alcohol. He was a heavy drinker, but one day while babysitting for them, he was working out in his garage, where he would repaint cars for people. He had come in and given me a beer. I thought it tasted pretty good, so I drank it. He gave me another and told me to hurry and drink it because his wife would be home soon. So I did. I started feeling "different". What did I know? He had taken me into his room and laid me on his bed and started fondling my breast and undoing my pants; he then proceeded to put his fingers in my vagina. When he had finished he told me I could go. I left, still feeling funny after having those two beers, and dirty too. It was raining out so I walked up to the school and swung on the swing for awhile, and then I went home. The first time I disclosed this I was fourteen or fifteen and I told my older sister Martha and a girlfriend what had happened. I decided to confront his wife and they went with me. His wife told me I was a liar and that all I wanted to do was cause problems. So I just let it go, because I thought it was entirely my fault. I had carried a lot of guilt. Years later I confronted him at a bar about what he did and how it ruined my life; at first he denied it, but he came back later and apologized for it. He never asked for forgiveness so I'm not sure if he really meant it or not. I don't even know if he did it to anyone else but more than likely he did. If they do it to one, then they usually try it with others.

My oldest sister Mary and I had gone to a Baptist preacher and told him what was happening and he had called mom to have her come to his office so we could talk about the sexual abuse going on between me and my brothers. She didn't want to hear any part of it. I had my sister take me to the emergency room because at that time I wanted to commit suicide. Thankfully, while I was there I met a nice nurse who took the time and just listened to me. We talked for hours and I left feeling better. Counseling was never recommended, as far as I know, or any type of medications from the hospital; they just let me go. I don't remember what she had said to me, but we have remained friends. Even today we still talk and see each other. I don't know if it had to be reported to Child Protective Services, but no one ever came to talk to me. Maybe the laws were different back then.

When I was fourteen I took on a summer job babysitting for a friend of my mother's who lived out of town. They worked at the same place and they worked the same shift. So sometimes they rode together. I was their live-in babysitter so I could earn some money for school clothes and I started the school year there. While living there, I was introduced to other girls my age and some older girls that I hung out with, as they were more mature. One night one of the girls I was hanging with and her boyfriend, who were both eighteen and old enough to drink before the law changed, asked me if I wanted to go out with them drinking. I told them sure. After all I already knew how to drink, I learned from my dad and the neighbor who were professionals. They had bought me a bottle of Strawberry Hill wine; it tasted sweet so I liked it. I must have liked it because I drank the whole bottle. Then they decided to pick up one of their friends for me who was eighteen, maybe older. We all went driving around and ended up on a hill that overlooked the town. I remember that part and the part where this older man had my pants down a little bit and his hand in my private area. When I returned to the trailer where I was living and babysitting, my mom's friend was waiting for me. She called my mom that night because I had come home drunk and had a hickey on my neck that was as big as a quarter, and the next day she had taken me back home. I guess my parents were pissed off at me. I don't remember too much of what happened to me for my consequences. I was supposed to be grounded, but I was able to hang around with my friends around town.

In March I think my mother had talked to her sister and brother-in-law in California. She had come to me and told me I was going to California to live and help take care of her sister who was dying of cancer. My mother, my sister Martha, and I all left for California. While there, I talked my sister Martha into staying there with me while my mom went back to New York. We both went to school while living out there. I was going to the middle school which consisted of seventh through ninth graders and Martha was going to the high school downtown, so she walked to school. I was the only white girl in my class and on the bus. The Mexicans would throw straight pins at me on the bus and harass me at school, so I just quit going to school. Nobody from the school called or said anything.

My aunt passed away just after Easter, but Martha and I decided to stay in California. My uncle would shower us with gifts, take us to Vegas, and just spend money on us. One night we all went out to a spaghetti dinner, then to the drive-in to watch a movie, I think it was *Worms*. The only reason why I can remember this is because it all went hand in hand. We had spaghetti for dinner and the movie just happened to be called worms. Anyhow Martha sat up front during the movie and I was in the back sitting on a big stack of carpet. During a break between movies, Martha and I had to go to the bathroom. When we got out, I noticed her pants were undone. I didn't say anything. We got back home and we all sat on the couch watching a movie; our uncle sat between the both of us. I don't know what he was doing with her at this time, but with me he had his hands in my pants. I got up and went to bed; I didn't feel comfortable with the whole situation. The next morning I got up and Martha wasn't in bed, so I got up and saw her in bed with our uncle Chris, who was only our uncle by marriage. I was upset with her, I don't know why really. What they were doing didn't bother her because she thought it was okay they were doing this. I had slapped her and told her I was going to run away. I guess because I let everyone abuse me I didn't want her to let it happen to her. I didn't know if she was molested as a child or not, but I didn't want her to feel obligated with sex like I did.

After she left for school that day, I walked over to a cousin's house and told them what was going on. They told me it was none of my business and to stay out of it. Evidently I said the wrong thing because my cousin hauled off and cracked me along side my face. I thought I was going to go flying through her sliding glass doors. I stayed with my cousin who had hit me as I had no other place to go. I didn't want to go back to Martha and Chris' home. After a few months it got to the point where they said I was causing trouble for everyone and they sent me back to New York.

At the age of fifteen I was back living at home again and back in school. There were seven of us left at home. I decided to put all my effort into sports. Because my mom worked a lot, I took on the role of keeping the house cleaned, doing the cooking and laundry for the kids, and trying to keep up with my schoolwork as I was the oldest girl at home. My mom had told me she was having an affair with a man at work. At this point it didn't matter to me; heck, my dad did it, so it was like, "whatever." One night she had asked me to take a bag of clothes around the house and put it on the porch. She had told my dad that she was working overtime and got dressed for work like any other workday. I don't know why she thought she had to tell me everything, maybe she felt compelled or something. My mom left and my dad who had already been drinking was angry again, saying she wasn't going to work, she was going to meet her boyfriend and how she was a bitch and a whore. I was sitting in a small chair by the television and the rest of the kids were sitting on the couch all lined up watching a movie, I don't know if they had heard the conversation my father was having with me about mom. When my dad came over, he put his arm around my shoulders so his hand would dangle. While touching and fondling my one breast he told me, "If your mother can whore around, so can you." He had asked me to go into his bedroom. I remember just sitting there not saying anything and he left to go to bed. I went upstairs to bed. The next day I had turned to a schoolteacher and told her what had happened. She or someone from the school must have reported it because the principal had called me up to the office after school and there were two police officers there. I had to tell them what had happened. They said they knew my father and they would handle the situation. There was no police report made up because they knew us. I found that information out after my oldest sister went and asked to see the report. My mom wasn't too happy with me now. She had to send me to Pennsylvania for two weeks at her friend's house until my dad left the house. He was mandated to leave the house. While staying with my mom's friend, mom had brought her boyfriend over there for me to meet. His name was Frank and seemed to be a nice guy. Dad had moved to Texas to stay with Nancy and her boyfriend. Nancy is an older sister of mine; she is five years older than me. In the months to follow, my mom spent her time working or going out with her friends. Once she had brought one girlfriend over when they were stopping to take a potty break before going to another bar. I had made chili for dinner and they dumped a beer in it. It made me angry to think they put the beer in the chili because they weren't the ones eating it. I had made it for us kids. Who wants to eat chili with beer in it? I'm not sure if we ate it or not.

In May of 1977 my sophomore year at school, my dad came home to visit us kids. It was late at night and my mom was working the late shift. He just stopped in for a few minutes, didn't say too much, but told me to call mom at work and let her know he was there. So I did. He knew she was going to call the police, so he left before they arrived. When they arrived they checked out the house and saw he was gone so they left. The next day I had a softball game out of town and when we arrived at the school after the game everyone was able to get off the bus except me; I had to stay on. The coach from the boys' team had told my coach to let me know that my father was dead. He had committed suicide. I felt numb; I couldn't believe he did that. Talk about guilt.

My oldest sister, Jean, who denies it to this day, told me it was my fault he did this. We were at a Memorial Day function at the Catholic Church and walking together when she told me, but she says she doesn't remember saying it. I do, I can see us, and we were walking slowly around the grounds. I was feeling sad and depressed that day. But hey, maybe she doesn't remember. I certainly haven't forgotten it. There were a lot of mixed emotions going on in the house after that day. We all felt sad to have lost our father but at the same time relief, only because we wouldn't have to put up with the abuse anymore. I had five younger siblings and I could feel their loss of not having a father as they were so young maybe 8 or 9 and they became mom's protector I don't know how the older siblings who were married and out of the house felt.

The last two years of school I just existed, especially my senior year. I was heavy into drinking; I don't even know how I managed to graduate except for the help of my baby sister who was smart. I remember telling my mom I thought I had a drinking problem, but she disagreed. I believed her and just kept going on my way. I wanted to believe everything she said. I would drink, get drunk and just cry all the time. I never doubted her or asked her questions because I thought she was always right. The first and only time I talked back to her was when her boyfriend was visiting her and I was upset. I told her she never had time for us kids anymore and that she spent most of her time with her boyfriend and drinking. She came walking across the floor really fast and slapped me across the face. Wow, that hurt. After about an hour she decided to ask me to talk. Well, by then, it was too late. But I forgave her because I wanted to believe she didn't mean to hit me.

My mother had a lot of control over me. Whatever she wanted I would give her or do for her. It didn't matter what the consequences were. Without asking me she signed me up for a teen pageant; I didn't want to do this because I thought I was ugly, but it was too late for me to drop out, and of course she never mentioned why she signed me up for this pageant. So I went. My mom had gotten a hand-me-down yellow dress for this event. I remember seeing all the other girls; they were pretty and smart, so why did she put me in this event? I remember walking up the aisle and tripping over my gown. It was embarrassing and to top it off during the interview part they asked me some science question and I was clueless. I just made a comical thing out of it because I was good at being a clown. After all, I was always a class clown. Another time she and her boyfriend signed me up for a mud-wrestling contest. When we got to the place for this contest we were late and I had to take on the champion who weighed 165 lbs, while I weighed maybe 115 lbs. Sure, I won, but you know I didn't do it for me. I did it for my mom because I wanted her to love me like she did the other kids. All my life I was trying to please her and I couldn't and yet whenever she needed anything, if I had it, I would give it to her.

When I graduated from high school, one of my older sisters was graduating from a religious college so my mom spent her money on my sister's graduation dinner. My mom treated us all to dinner out that night and then the money we used for my graduation I took out of my social security I was getting for my dad's death to help pay for my party. It was okay with me because my mom needed it. That same year I was able to buy my first pair of jeans. .

A year after I graduated I moved back to California with my sister Martha and her husband (our late aunt's husband). He would always tell me he was my dad because I had his nose. I went and asked my mom and she said no. But to this day I sometimes wonder if he was. I had found a good-paying job working at a prestigious country club. Members consisted of millionaires, movie stars and President Ford. My self-esteem was still very low; I felt worthless but still put on a happy face. I was making good money so I was able to get my own apartment. Living on my own seemed to make matters worse because it gave me too much time to really dwell on the negative thoughts I was feeling about myself.

I had always let my sister Martha have control over me. If she didn't like an outfit that I was going to buy for myself, I wouldn't buy it. I went shopping with her one day and bought all the clothes that she liked and some shoes. Even if I didn't like them, I would buy them because she liked them. For years I let her control me, now I am finally able to let go and stand on my own. But it has taken me years.

There was a bar where I always hung out after work and I became friends with the owner who was the bartender as well. He would introduce me to everyone as his daughter. One night he introduced me to this guy who was looking for a partner to dance with at the nearby disco for a contest. Well, I loved to dance so I said sure. We did a few dances and found we were good together. He stated that we should go back to my place and put a few things together for our routine. I went along with it, and on the way there he suggested we pick up a bottle of red wine, so we did. We got back to my place and he had asked me to put on a long skirt that would twirl when he spun me around because I had on my work uniform. While I was in changing, he poured us a glass of wine. I came out and he told me to take a sip to relax me. I did and that was all I remember until I was driving to my girlfriend's home all upset. She wasn't home, of course; they had gone out of town. I don't know how long I had been out and I don't know where the guy went. I never saw him again. I can't even tell you what had happened to me. I was unconscious the whole time or for how ever long it lasted.

The next day I went into the bar and told the owner what had happened. He said he really didn't know the guy that well, but for me to go get checked out. I called the doctor, but he said there wasn't anything he could do for me; he didn't check for any disease. I never even thought that I could have gotten pregnant by this guy. So I let it slip to the back of my mind. I guess it was just another one of those things that was supposed to happen to me. Needless to say, I ended up moving back in with my sister again because I was scared to live alone after that incident.

Months later the same bartender introduced me to another man. He was 6'4", good looking, had a beautiful smile and seemed to be really nice. We dated and I thought I finally met Mister Right. His name was Hugh. We soon got engaged. He was very thoughtful, he would send me dozens of roses all the time and we would go out in a limousine and have the driver take us all around. Almost as soon as I agreed to marry him I started backing away from him. I guess I was afraid of commitment. I had pushed him away, but we would still date from time to time and make love. Since he paid for everything I felt obligated to him so therefore we would have sex. I ended up pregnant by him and then the nightmares began. I wanted a baby so I could have someone to love who would love me back and not hurt me. Hugh would chase me down all the time. One night he sent a limo driver to pick me up because he said my life was in danger and of course I believed him. The driver took me to a hotel where Hugh was waiting for me. He told me to stay there and that he would be right back. A few hours later he came back, but his chest was all cut up and when I asked what had happened he wouldn't tell me. He just said not to worry about it, that everything would be all right. I didn't know he was into drugs at this time, I didn't know much about drugs until later in life. I ran home to New York and there in September of 1985 I gave birth to a baby boy I named Michael.

I couldn't find a job here that paid enough for me to support us, so I returned to California with my son and continued working and raising Michael. When I left Hugh he knew I was pregnant and he never tried to contact us. He was already in a new relationship with another woman. I did call him at work and let him know he had a son. There was no contact with Michael's dad, but his aunt Lynn and I always kept in contact. One day she called and wanted to know if I would bring Michael over and let his dad see him. I thought about it and decided to let him see his son, but I wouldn't let him see him or us alone. We met at Lynn's house. He wanted to get back together. I thought that maybe Hugh had changed and that my son needed a father so I took him back. It didn't last long. My mom came out to visit us and while she was there I didn't dare to sleep with Hugh. I don't know why. My mom kept saying go get in bed. I wouldn't leave the living room. Even growing up I would never bring a guy to our house to meet my family, so I'm thinking it had a lot to do with the way I grew up. A few days after my mom left to go back home, Hugh came home drunk, and he started throwing things. He tried to rip off my mother's ring that my mother had bought me, saying it was from another man. I just laid frozen on the floor hanging on to Michael. I was afraid Hugh would grab him from me and take the only thing that I really loved in the world. I didn't dare move until I knew Hugh was passed out. When I knew he was asleep, I called my cousin and told her if I wasn't at her house in ten minutes to come looking for me. I had left a note for Hugh, stating I wanted him out of my home before I got back from work. I had come home in between shifts to see if he had left and he had. There were a lot of empty champagne bottles lying all over and papers all over the place. I don't know if he and his friends drank them or just dumped them. Either way it was a big mess. I turned around and went right back out the door. I left to go back to work and when I was sitting at a red light I saw him jump out of a car and run after me. I locked my car doors and the light turned green, so I just stepped on the gas and left. That was the last time we had contact with Michael's father. Nine years later Hugh was killed in a drug-related incident. But we continue to have communication with Hugh's sister Lynn who has always been there for Michael.

Because of the sexual abuse I encountered growing up, when I left home and for many years to follow; I put myself into predicaments where the abuse would continue, not realizing still that it all had to do with my past. Here is another example of an incident that I put myself into. One time going to Vegas with Martha and her husband we had a couple of beers on the way there. When we got there, they went to their room and I went to the black jack table, where I met a man. We drank and the next thing I knew I was in his room. When I woke up he was fastening my pants and there were four other guys there. To this day I wonder if I was a victim of date rape. I was angry for putting myself into that situation without realizing what was going on, but it was a pattern with me all my life.

I know people will say, "You were an adult, you should have known better, or you could have stopped it." Well, they are wrong because research says the behavior stems from your childhood and what your childhood was like. Do you think I liked the person I was on those occasions? Not really, but I didn't care about *me* then.

When you're told over and over again to just lie there and take it or are threatened, then that's all you know. You carry all of that with you all your life. It's a learned behavior that was instilled in me as I was growing up.

Am I proud about all the situations I put myself into? Absolutely not. I wouldn't wish them on anyone. I'm more embarrassed than anything, but I can't change the past, I can only learn from it.

When I look back on my childhood, it looks like everything was a chain reaction. It's like I was passed around from family members, to friends of my brothers, and fathers of the kids I used to babysit for. The events that happened helped shape me into what I was to become in my adult life. As long as I let them have their way with me, then I was led to believe I was doing the right thing as an adult. I was starving for some attention and the sex was the only way I knew to get that. I didn't know anything about having a relationship or how to be in one. All I knew was how to drink and get drunk to numb myself so I wouldn't feel anything they were doing to me, and to let them have their way with me, and not to anger them to the extent of physical abuse.

When I reflect back on my feelings toward my parents, it's hard for me to really blame them, but they knew. They knew all about it. I told my mom about everything and she chose to ignore it. But I still loved her. I forgive them because they thought they were doing the best they knew how raising us kids. I hated my father because of the violence he showed toward my family and what he did to me. I hated the fact that he had a lot of women he was seeing and didn't try to hide it. He had his favorites among the kids as well as my mom had hers, and guess what, I wasn't one of them. I was the one always in trouble or supposedly causing trouble for everyone in the family. Most of the time, I felt sorry for my mom. I felt like I had to be her protector as well as that for some of the other kids, especially my sisters because I didn't want the boys molesting my sisters as well.

I had always put my mom on a pedestal. I thought she could do no wrong; trying to get my mother's love and acceptance blinded me to the extent that I didn't care about all the wrong things she was doing. It didn't matter what it was, I still thought of her as perfect. There are some things that had happened with my mom, but after working through it in therapy I just let it go. I don't really remember what it all was and that is fine as long as it is dealt with and processed.

I don't feel anger towards my mom. I'm not sure why I'm not angry, because I told her about the sexual abuse and she didn't do anything about it. It's strange that I *should* be mad, but I'm not.

Part II

I met my husband Joe through his mother. I met her at a bar where she was playing in a band. She was a musician and played the bass. Joe and I dated off and on, but nothing too serious. Then I needed to find a place to rent because they had sold the place where I was living. Judy, who was to eventually become my mother-in-law, offered to rent a room to me since she had a three-bedroom home and needed the money. I thought it would be okay, so my son Michael and I moved in.

Joe and I started dating again after I moved in to his mom's house. Then after a while we made it more official and switched the bedrooms. We were living together as a couple. We had talked marriage, but I wasn't ready yet. I had gotten pregnant and Joe had started to get into drugs again. I don't know if it's because I was pregnant or if he just had to get that fix. There were a lot of different nights he wouldn't come home and then the next day when he did come home I didn't have to question anything because his mother and grandmother would jump on him. I found it strange that they would interfere with our relationship like that, but I didn't say anything. I thought it was normal. They were always putting their voices in on everything. After a while I was tired of the whole situation and left Joe and came back to New York. In August of 1989 I had a beautiful baby boy whom my mother named David. I called Judy, his grandmother, to let her know the baby had been born. We talked and she convinced me to come back out there with my sons. Joe was living out of the house and in with his new girlfriend. As soon as I returned to California I went back to work again and Judy babysat while I worked days. Judy and I began to bond more like mother and daughter. She was having problems with paying her bills and things and so I would turn my checks over to her. I was giving her control of my life and not realizing it at this point.

I started dating a bartender that I was working with named Mike. He seemed really nice and caring. He was at my house one day when I had to leave to take my oldest son Michael to visit his father at his

Aunt Lynn's house. I had taken David and Michael with me as Judy had some other plans that day. Mike said his friend was coming over to pick him up, so he would be leaving a few minutes after me. I returned a few hours later to find him and Judy lying on the floor. When I walked in, they saw me and she leaned over and whispered something to him. I thought that the whole thing didn't look right at all. He said his friend forgot to pick him up. To this day I don't know if anything happened between them, but you know what they say: go with your gut instincts.

I continued to live with Joe's mom. At this time I wasn't having a lot of contact with my family. She had convinced me that my family was trying to control me. She was actually the controlling one, but I didn't see that coming yet.

Months later she convinced me to try and get Joe back. I thought I still loved him; I mean, he is so intelligent and all. What I fell in love with was his brain. I thought my kids would be smart because he is smart. She thought it best we get back together for the baby's sake. So I agreed. I went every Friday and Saturday night after work to see him. There were times he wouldn't say anything. Then one night he asked me to wait for him after work; I thought I had him back that night. Instead we made love and I got pregnant again for the second time by him. He said he would call me. He never did. I found out the girl he was living with was three months pregnant ahead of me, so I decided just to let it go because it was evident he wasn't ready to leave her because of his drug problem. Judy kept on me to keep going up there and seeing him. I think she just wanted him home to get control of him again. Then a month before I had my third son, Joseph, his mother told me that Joe had gotten married. Then she played this game, "I thought you knew." She knew, but it just seemed she forgot to tell me. She also convinced me to quit my job at the country club and work at the hotel where she was playing music.

Two years later Joe came back home to be with his mom. He had walked out on his wife and daughter, then found out she was pregnant by him again. It turned out to be another girl. He was put in a rehab place for thirty days. We went to see him when we could. Joe and I started talking more and I thought we could make it work. I wanted my kids to have their father in their lives. It was going pretty well until he came home from rehab and then things began to change. His mom would make arrangements for someone to go with her to watch his wife's apartment and see if there was anything going on there that shouldn't be happening. I went once and didn't like the idea of it. I started to get scared because now she was bound and determined to try and take her granddaughters away from their mother one way or another. She would document whatever she saw. There were a lot of days Joe's mom would go to the town where the grandchildren lived and look for some evidence to try and get the girls. I felt sorry for his wife then.

Things in our relationship seemed to have been getting worse. Joe and his mom would take off and go all the time. One time we were to go Christmas shopping together, just Joe and me, but instead he and his mom went. One day I just left because I knew it wouldn't work as long as she was living with us. I got another apartment for the kids and me not too far from where she lived so the kids could still visit them. But in the back of my mind I always had this fear that she would take my kids away from me. Joe and I still dated, (he was divorced from his first wife) and sometimes he would spend the night and just hang out with us. Then one day in May 1994 my sister passed away in New York from cancer, I made arrangements for Joe and his mother to keep the three kids while I was gone for the funeral. I got back and they said they were going to Mexico for a week. I didn't think anything of it so I said okay; a few days after they left I was served with visitation papers from their lawyer stating that Joe and I would trade every other weekend and holidays to have the kids. Therefore it was their weekend to have the kids. They came and picked them up right on time. I couldn't believe it; to make things worse they had told their lawyer I was out of town on vacation. I should have known she was up to something, because Joe would never have even thought that up. His mom always did his thinking for him.

Since I didn't like this idea at all I wasn't sure what to do. Then in August I found out I was pregnant yet again. This time I had a girl, Judith in March of 1995. Again the same thing happened. I moved in with Joe and his mom because I wasn't about to let the kids go over there and let their grandmother fill their minds with crap. I wanted to be right there when she was near them. Judy had lost her house and we were all living with Joe's grandmother. From there we moved all over. We moved to Sacramento, then back to Palm Springs. While we were there I had finally decided to marry Joe as Judy thought it was best that we all had the same last name except for Michael. We were married in August of 1996 in Palm Desert, California; then in February of 1997 we decided to move to Florida and in August of 1997 we moved to New York.

We had seven kids: I had one son by a previous relationship, three kids with my husband and then we had his ex-wife's three kids as she lost custody because of her drug problem. We were given custody of her three kids in 1995. We were staying with my sister Maryanne in Hornell at the time since we had just moved up to New York from Florida because Joe had a good job lined up before we left Florida in 1997.

In late August 1997 I found out my husband, now my ex-husband, had been molesting our children. I noticed my two-year-old daughter started wetting her pants again, so I had to put her back in diapers. When her dad would pick her up, she would scream. I didn't think much of it until one time on a hot August night. I started to go into the living room and my husband and his seven-year-old daughter Danielle were sitting on the couch. She was on his lap and they had a blanket over them. I told the kids it was so nice out that they should go outside and play. They all went outdoors; including my husband, and then Danielle came back in and said she had to go to the bathroom. She said that her puttee hurt. I asked her what her father was doing under the blankets and she said that her dad had his fingers in her puttee. I wasn't sure what to do at first. I knew I had to report this because I didn't want this to be on going for her as it had been for me.

That night I took Danielle to the police station where we met with a CPS worker. I told Joe that we were just going to the store for a few minutes. The CPS worker had taken Danielle into another room without me to talk to her alone. There they had an anatomically correct doll and she proceeded to tell the CPS worker and the police officer what had been happening to her. They came out and told me to take the kids out of the home until they could make an arrest. They said it would take a couple of days. In the meantime I had to figure out how to get my younger two boys back from California. Joe and I had let their grandmother take them just so she wouldn't have to make the trip from Florida to California alone. She wasn't going to move to New York with us as she decided she didn't like New York.

I told my husband that the boys had to get back because we needed to get them settled before school started. He called his mom and she said she would meet me in Texarkana at the train station. I told my husband that since he was working the kids could stay with my sister June. He agreed because he wasn't much for watching the kids.

My sister's husband Terry and I arrived in Texarkana, picked up the kids, and drove straight back without stopping. When we got back they still hadn't arrested my husband. I called the police to see what was happening; they told me to make something up so he wouldn't get suspicious. This was on going for a little over a week. So I told my husband that I had found us an apartment and was fixing it up for him, and that when I got done I would let him know. I told him it would only be for a couple more days. He believed me. A week later he was arrested and sent to the Steuben County jail. He was arrested for child molestation. He was in jail till the court date at which time he had to have proof of a place of residency. He was able to come up with the money to move into the Days Inn and after a week he had found a place to live in another small city about an hour away where he still lives. After that his mom had come out and helped him out. At one point I started to feel sorry for him, but I couldn't let it get the best of me because I was worried that the girls would end up growing up like me. I lost 25 lbs. in a month and to top it off my past images of sexual abuse started recurring.

I found a house where the kids and I could live. My mother-in-law came out from California to help her son and had no place to stay, so I offered to let her stay with us and baby-sit the kids while I worked. At this time I had started drinking more and working a lot as an assistant manager for a store. I had CPS case workers visiting once a week to see how the kids were doing. They recommended that I go for counseling so I agreed. I knew I needed it.

One day I came home after work and my mother-in-law was getting ready to go out and meet her son. I noticed she had a piece of paper in her hand. She was writing something, and then put it back in her dresser. I thought it was strange; I remembered she used to do that to keep tabs on Joe's first wife, so I checked it out and sure enough she was keeping tabs on my comings and goings. Documenting everything. She was trying to get enough on me to try and take my kids away. She figured that since I turned her son in for sexual abuse that she would try to prove me unfit. It was driving me nuts. The next day I called my therapist all worked up. We talked and decided I needed to go into the hospital for a few days. We called my CPS caseworker to let her know what was going on. I told my manager at work where I was going and they laid me off from my job because

I went in the hospital. I don't think it was legal at the time, but that is what they did. Judy said she would watch the kids while I was in the hospital. While in there I had time to get my priorities straight. I also had nightmares about my husband and mother-in-law. The dreams were pointing things out to me. I could see a clear picture of what my life was like, the things Joe and Judy did to me. I was able to see things for what they really were. Before I was able to leave the hospital, we set up a meeting with my mother in-law to discuss my husband, her son. It seems that she was blaming me for what my husband did. A lot of the time he would fall asleep on the couch and I would just let him sleep there, so she was saying we didn't sleep together all the time and weren't having enough sex. Like she would know what happened in our room. So she left angry and blaming me. I was in the hospital for a week before I was able to come home. When I did return home, I called and set up my next appointment to see my therapist.

I returned home and things were getting worse. My sister June and her husband decided to put a trailer on their land for the kids and me to move into. They said it would be done by June. At this point my mother-in-law and I were fighting and I thought the only way to get her out of my life was to give her custody of the three stepkids. I had to file court papers for this action, but the day we went to court, thinking she would get the kids, my lawyer pulled me to the side and said there was no way they were going to give her custody. She told me that after I left the court I should just go finish loading the trucks and move into the trailer. My mother-in-law knew she wasn't going to get the kids after I came back from talking to my lawyers. The judge had said no. I actually felt sorry for her, but she didn't get the kids.

After we lived in the trailer for about three months the kids started to feel more comfortable and safe. When the Child Protective Workers came out for a home visit, three of the kids told them about being molested by their father and two of the other boys opened up and told them they had seen them being touched by their father. When I took the kids down to the investigators to file a report, we had problems with one of the girls not wanting to talk about it.

Now I had everyone in therapy. I had a two-year-old going through her issues of not letting me out of her sight, a four-year-old going through a lot of anger and wanting to sit on men's laps inappropriately, two six-year-olds, (a boy who had anger problems and a girl who went into a shell and wouldn't talk), and then three older boys who were confused about everything going on in our lives. Then there was me with my issues, so it was crazy a lot of the times. Since I wasn't working I focused on keeping everybody's appointments in order and making sure they went to all of them, including my therapy and alcohol counseling appointments. I didn't care about anything except keeping all of our appointments because I wanted to make sure my kids wouldn't have to go through what I went through growing up, not having the help I needed to heal.

After awhile it was beginning to take its toll on me. I loved all the kids the same, but I didn't have enough time in a day to give each of the kids the attention he or she should have, so I called their mother and found out that she had just gotten out of rehab. We talked and she was able to prove to the courts that she was clean so the courts gave her back custody of the kids. She came to New York to pick them up. She stayed for a couple of days and we were able to talk and clear the air between us and became the best of friends. I was a little concerned on how the kids would react. At first we were all upset because we had grown close as a whole family. Then after my stepkids' mother came it had sunk in. They were leaving and we would never see them again. My own kids went into another room and held in their tears. I hugged them and told them it was okay to cry and show their feelings. My step children were sad to leave but were happy to be going home with their real mom. This was in 1999 and we didn't hear from them after that, until 2002 when their mother ended up in the hospital and the Palm Springs, California CPS unit called me. The children ended up in foster care until a relative of mine was able to get them. She lived in the same state and county they did, where as I live in New York, so it was easier for them to stay there. My niece now has permanent custody of them and has recently moved. I don't hear much from them, but I know they are being well taken care of. Meanwhile my uncle Bill babysat for me while I worked and sometimes he would take the kids to his house on the lake to go swimming and my daughter who was three at the time told me that he had touched her puttee. I thought, oh no, here we go again. I called CPS and they brought her in to talk to her and then my uncle Bill (by marriage). They had claimed that it was unfounded, but it still sticks in the back of my mind so I don't leave her alone with him. He comes around a lot and does a lot for me and my kids which

I do appreciate it, but the trust has been broken. He comes around a lot to try and get into my family system. He wants us to be in a relationship and get married, but I don't see him as a boyfriend or lover, I see him as my uncle and always will.

Through all these years my mother-in-law and my ex-husband have never had respect for me. They always treated me like I was stupid. I was told what to do and I would do as I was told. I never questioned any of it. I didn't say anything to anyone because every time I confronted her about anything she would say I was crazy. I believed her. She had control over everyone in the house, sometimes even her own mother when she lived with her. I wouldn't do anything unless I went through her first. I believed everything she said.

However, she has given up trying to ruin my life. I thought we had heard the last from her, but in just the past few weeks she has managed to find my son David's email address (through My Space, I believe) and she is contacting him. He shows me all of the messages and his responses. He and I have discussed this with our counselor. David says he is fine with the situation, but very wary of her attempts to get back into his life. As far as my ex-husband goes, we never see or hear from him and we don't want to have contact with him. He never got jail time for what he did; he was only given five years probation and counseling. He has finished his probation , but has made no attempts to contact us; that's a good thing.

Part III

When I first realized I needed help I went to four different counselors. The first was a psychologist; I only saw him once, I didn't feel comfortable with him. The second one was a man also; I saw him maybe twice, which didn't work out either. The third was a lady from church; she seemed to be more worried about getting her money than about my problems, so I quit going to her. The fourth lady I was introduced to by my mother-in-law and she seemed to think that my mother-in-law and I were lovers in our past lives. I went to her a couple of times. I thought this was all nuts so I gave up until years later when I was ready to try another therapist. I didn't want to think that all therapists were the same, so when CPS recommended me to Mental Health. I was relieved because I knew I needed the help and I didn't want to give up or go on thinking they were all alike. I had tried so many and when I finally met the right one it was great. So you see you can't give up just because you run into a few bad eggs. Keep searching because it is worth it once you've found the one that you feel can help you. You need to feel comfortable with a therapist. Someone you can trust and respect.

I finally found the right one after my kids' sexual abuse came out. She is wonderful. She is honest, caring and great to work with. When I first went in to see her I was scared and alone. My self-esteem was so low it was dragging on the ground. I thought I was ugly and didn't deserve to be loved by anyone. I went in thinking I was crazy because my mother-in-law always told me I was crazy and I thought I was heading in that direction because of the flashbacks I was having. I had flashbacks of my brother raping me, and touching me inappropriately. But I also went in knowing I needed help and no matter what, I was going to get it. I wasn't going to give up.

After meeting with my therapist for the first time, she only asked a few questions and when I left I remember thinking, "Is this it? Is this what my therapy was going to be all about?" So I decided to go to my next appointment. I returned the next week and together we worked on my family tree and it was a big tree. We talked a little about my family and where I fit in the tree.

She had given me a book to read, *Working with Your Inner Child*. I couldn't wait to get started. So as soon as I got home I went to work on it because that was my first sign of hope. I wanted all the knowledge that I could get. Throughout my therapy I would look for some self-help books and they were the only books I would read. I had picked up Dave Pelzer's books and read them; they were an inspiration to me. And I knew if he could work through his trauma, then I could succeed as well.

One thing I learned about therapy is that you have to want it bad enough to succeed. You have to go through the process, not around it, under it, or over it: you need to go through it. Is it fun? Heck no, and it's not easy either. It's a lot of hard work and determination on the client's part. First and most importantly is that you need to feel safe and comfortable with your therapist. I feel mine was a God send. I'm always thankful for her, because if it weren't for the bond I have with her, I wouldn't be where I am today. Secondly, you need to be open and honest with your therapist and thirdly, don't be ashamed of yourself. What happened to you was not your fault.

Therapy takes time. It could take up to five years or more. But if you really want to get better and healthier then time doesn't matter. There are times when it can be very intense because you are bringing up the past and at the same time old feelings come with it. But after you work with the feelings it gets better. That is how it is with everything you deal with. There were times when I said I was not going back, but the following week I was back in there, because I was tired of living in the same cycle that I had been living in and I didn't want my kids growing up and repeating that cycle as well. I needed to get over the past and the only way to do that is to just keep going to all of my weekly or bi-weekly appointments. I wanted things in my life to change for the better. I kept picking the same type of men to have a relationship. They were men that drank all the time or did drugs. If they were serious and they asked me to marry them I would say yes, then the next day I would push the men away. I was afraid to love someone and even now I know it wasn't true love. None of my relationships were. Sure I loved them the only way I knew how and I guess they didn't know how to love either. That's not normal. Love is wanting to be with someone for the rest of your life.

There are going to be a lot of times when you feel down during therapy, especially when you start talking about your past abuse and that's when a lot of women drop out of therapy. Women tend to drop out because they can't handle or are afraid to work on their feelings of what happened to them as a child. Then they end up living their same type of life over and over. Their behavior patterns didn't change and they don't understand why things are still the same. They didn't give themselves time to dig deep enough to get to the root of the problem. It can be very scary examining issues "face to face." It takes a great deal of courage and determination to get through it.

To me therapy was like breaking down every part of me and rebuilding someone who loves and appreciates herself and who has her own opinions and thoughts. I have learned to love and respect myself. What others think about me is their problem.

You can make it if you want to badly enough, but it's up to you and the outcome is determined by how honest you are with yourself as well as with your therapist.

We did different types of treatments. One we did was EMDR, Eye Movement Desensitization and Reprocess. I would have headphones on and put a sensor in the palms of my hands, then with my eyes closed I would feel and hear a rhythm and at the same time my eyes would move back and forth. I would focus on a problem that I may remember vaguely and with the rhythms it helped bring the problem up. For example: I focused on a certain smell or parts of a flashback and it would bring it up. It's like riding on a train and it just goes by. It helped to process the information quicker than just talking about it. After I did these treatments I found that within a couple of days I would feel so much better. Without that treatment it would take a few days more, and the anxiety would last longer because it takes longer to process information when you just talk about it. There were times in therapy when I was working on my past abuse that I could smell semen, or my breast would leak when we talked about children or babies. I could also feel things, like for example: I was talking with my sister Jean one day about how my mother would slap us on the back when she would hit us and at that time I could literally feel it on my back. Before doing this type of treatment plan you need to learn coping skills such as going for a walk when the anxiety builds up, taking a hot bubble bath, talking to a friend or doing some journaling. I did a lot of journaling throughout my treatment plan and it helped because once it's on paper you can let it go till your next appointment.

I realized in therapy that what had happened to me wasn't my fault. But we go through life taking on the blame, and guilt, and shame of it because we are told it's all our fault as we grow up, while the abuser or abusers walk around thinking they did nothing wrong. Throughout your life they treat you like crap and make snotty remarks to keep your self-esteem down, just to make them think they still have control of you. But you can't give them that power; you need to take it back.

During therapy I realized I was going through life looking for a mother. Don't get me wrong, I loved my mother very much and would do anything for her, but it wasn't the same as what I have for my own children. My mom had a lot on her plate, besides raising all of us kids, so she did the best she knew how to do at that time. But even today I find sometimes that I'm still looking for that " perfect mother" and I know I'll never find her, but it's just something that I need to deal with. I was so set on looking for that "perfect mother" that relationships with men weren't important to me. I guess that's why I bonded so fast with my mother-in-law. I thought she was that "perfect mother". She treated me like her own daughter until the head games began. I married her son, whom I did love the only way I knew how, just to keep the bond between my mother-in-law and me. At one point in my life I was having a real hard time with my identity, am I gay or not because I was told that because I wasn't in a relationship most of the time that I must like women. At one point I was attracted to my mother-in-law because of this identity confusion that was going on and once in awhile I still ask myself that question because I still haven't found Mister Right. To make matters worse my family physician that I had been going to also questioned me and had me thinking maybe I am gay. She seemed to be more worried about my love life than my health. I went into see her one day and she said, "Lisa, you haven't been in a relationship in eight years. Don't you think you may be gay?" She told me to think about it and come see her in a week. Well, heck, I went to my therapist and talked to her because I thought maybe the doctor was right. After talking to my therapist I realized that I was told that I wasn't because I had already worked on my identity confusion a long time ago. I can't picture me having sex with other women; it just isn't me. I have nothing against the gay community, but it just isn't me.

I also learned a lot about myself in therapy. One thing is that I don't have to lie about anything especially my feelings, and it's so much easier and healthier for me. Just to be able to be honest with my kids and myself is great. I tell my kids everything. I don't hold anything back and my kids have a lot of respect for me because of the openness and bond we have. I am able to stand up for myself and if others don't like what I say, then that is their choice. We own our own feelings, thoughts and opinions; nobody can make us feel differently. We chose to feel the way we want.

I went through some times when I would stay up all night crying because I couldn't understand why these things happened to me. There were a lot of times I just wanted to drop therapy, but I wouldn't let myself give up. I wanted to learn why I did the things I did and why I let everyone hurt me while I was growing up. I had learned to bond with and love my kids from growing up watching TV shows like *The Brady Bunch* or similar shows that had parents showing their affection for their kids and talking honestly to them about life. I didn't have that, but I want that for my own children.

Once there was a time I was so depressed and crying constantly that I wasn't able to sleep, so

I turned on the TV. The show that was on was a psychic show, so I thought I would call them, in hopes of getting some answers about my life. I called and the next week I received my phone bill. I was shocked: the bill came to $500.00. I called the phone company to set up payment arrangements and told them what I had done. They worked with me and said normally people don't admit to doing this and they blame it on their kids. I told them, "Well, I could blame my kids, but it's my own doing not theirs." When I told my therapist about this, she couldn't believe I did this. I laugh about it today. But I also learned a lesson: stick to therapy--it's a lot cheaper. There were other times I would watch *Sister Act*. It would make me laugh, but also I felt a connection to it, because through all of this, I still had my faith. There were times I felt alone, but I know He was and is there.

I didn't have much of an outside support system, but I had my kids who were always there for me. We supported each other. It gave us the chance to get to know each other. There were times I would fix candlelight dinners so we could all sit and discuss how we were all feeling about different issues that would come up. I did have a lot of support from my therapist as well as my alcohol abuse counselor. If I needed a kick to get me on the right track, I would call my therapist and she would say the right thing to get me going again.

Once a week I would go to a group called "Adult Survivors of Sexual Abuse" with 9 other women . It was a very intense group. There were times when things got too hard to handle, but we all stuck with it. One night we had to bring to group a letter to our abusers. I had written one to my brother who raped me. I started to read mine. When I get really nervous, I laugh then I'll cry. I couldn't do it. I couldn't get through it. But I finally was able to read mine after a few of the others read theirs. We all supported each other and helped each other cope with the past. Another one of our assignments was to make an album with pictures and some drawings. That was hard to start because our first assignment was to draw a picture of ourselves and then our abuser(s). I had a hard time putting a face on mine as I didn't want to see the abusers. After we were done I burned up all the writing I had done to all of my abusers plus the album. I wish now that I had kept them, but I was afraid at that time that the wrong person might get it and read it.

During therapy I learned that if you don't admit to yourself what happened then it leaves self-doubt in your mind, but when you admit it out loud, then it becomes a reality. Talk about it. If you bond with your therapist and are comfortable with him or her, then you will realize that he or she is very understanding, that he/she does believe you and is very empathic. A therapist can't do your work for you, but that person is there to help you work through all your problems and guide you, but YOU have to want it for yourself, not for anybody else.

There were times I left my therapist's office so mad at her (because she was right on all accounts), but I didn't want to accept the facts. Then I would say, "I'm not going back." The next week would come up and yep I would be there right on time. There will be times we leave angry at out therapist, and it's okay to do that. Once you stop and think about why you're angry, it all makes sense. At the time it doesn't seem to because your mind is focusing on your anger, but it will come to you.

There were times when I needed a good jolt of reality and I would call my therapist. She would give me the right kick I needed to get back on the track to reality because sometimes things got to be so overwhelming that I would lose sight of what I was doing. There were days that it was hard to focus but again, if you have a good counselor you will succeed.

When I first started therapy she told me to call her if I needed to, so I did and then I felt so guilty I felt I had to send her flowers to apologize for bothering her. Back then I always felt guilty over everything. I did that a lot growing up because I didn't want anyone to hate me or dislike me, so it was one of my patterns throughout life.

I had my religious beliefs to help me as well. I would watch *Touched by an Angel* faithfully every week. To me I felt like it was my sermon and there was always a lesson to learn. Don't get me wrong, I went to a Baptist church, but in the particular church I went to it seemed like one family would run the whole thing, not the pastor. So my kids and I just quit going. I feel in God's house everyone gets treated the same. I guess it must reflect back on my childhood, because if you didn't have the right name then you weren't important. I've tried a Pentecostal church a couple of times, but didn't feel a sense of connection there either. The only church I went to and felt comfortable in was at a nondenominational church and there I always left feeling good about myself, because nobody there was singled out. They reached out to everyone and it didn't matter who or what you were. If only it was in New York instead of Palm Desert, California.

If you learn anything from this, I hope you learn that what happened to you as a child is not your fault. I know your abusers tell you all your life that it was, but IT'S NOT! You need to believe that. You are a worthwhile person and you are worth the time it takes to get help. Sure there will be times that you're afraid of being alone and that's okay; things are going to change and I know we are all afraid of change, but change can be good for you. You will learn who you really are and that's a great feeling. You will have the strength to stand up for yourself and think for yourself and that's a wonderful feeling to have control over your own life. One time I told my therapist that I felt like a flower with the petals getting ready to spread out and bloom and that's exactly how I felt because I was beginning to grow. I was beginning to love me.

You need to get mad, get angry at the ones who hurt you, who inflicted the pain on you. Write them a letter, tell them how they hurt you, express your thoughts and feelings, then later RIP IT UP and as you're ripping it up you can feel the anger leaving. You don't need to send it, but least you're getting it out of your system, releasing the hold the anger had on you.

When I was growing up we weren't allowed to show our feelings. In therapy is where I learned that it's okay to show affection for my kids. I learned how to talk to my kids and be honest with them. They know about my past of being sexually abused, they asked me who did it and I told them and they know that's the reason we don't attend very many family outings. Also, I wouldn't trust the relatives with my own kids. My children are very understanding and supportive of me. I had to explain to my kids that it was okay for them to show their feelings as well. That it's okay to cry and hug each other. When my three stepchildren went back to California, the kids went into their room to hide their feelings. I went in there and told them to cry because I knew they wanted to because I could tell by the looks on their faces. They were able to show their feelings without being made fun of. It opened the door for all of us as a family to bond even more. I told them to never be afraid to show their feelings.

Just a few years ago my oldest son went to give his aunt, one of my sisters, a hug and she wasn't sure how to respond because in her house they don't show their feelings. She tried to push him away. I told her don't be afraid to show your feelings, that it's okay to hug him. She laughed, but she did hug him.

My kids and I always say, "I love you" to each other. We say it all day long and we mean it. One day my son was in school and I had to take something to him and he gave me a hug and said, "I love you." He wasn't ashamed or embarrassed. He will do it in public when he's at work; that's how close we are.

Like I said, we don't hang around my family much. I sometimes wish we had a "perfect family," but they are only in storybooks or on television. During the holidays it's the worst for me, but I've learned to enjoy the time with my own children. When we put up our Christmas tree and decorate it, it seems like nothing else matters because we all have each other and we enjoy each other's company. Sure I wish we could be with my extended family, but I won't put myself in a situation where it is going to affect my self-esteem or hurt my kids. If your abuser gets one little chance to knock you down, he or she is going to do it, so why put myself in that situation. It's unhealthy for one thing and I'm worth much more than that. Today I am in charge of my own feelings and emotions. As we go through life we need to know we are always in control of how we think or feel. People can't make us think or feel a certain way, only we can. We have control over that. We need to take and keep that control.

My main point is, it doesn't matter if you've been abused once or more than once, abuse is abuse and you don't have to go through it alone. There is help for you, but you have to want it to be successful, and know you are worth it. I THINK YOU'RE WORTH IT!

Part IV

Today, I'm healthier than I've ever been. I have an open and honest relationship with my kids. We talk about everything from sex to whatever they want to know. Whatever the subject they bring up, we discuss it. I don't want my kids to ever feel like they can't talk to me about life; we put our cards on the table and we don't leave until everyone's opinion is discussed. Sure there are times when there are disagreements and we have our share of problems but, without the good communications we have and the love, we wouldn't be a happy family.

I'm still in therapy every four weeks and working on a few things, like how to be a part of a healthier relationship with people and my panic attacks that I sometimes have when I drive, usually when there is bad weather. Before I started this I had found a wonderful friend who has been a great support for me. Actually she was a friend all along and I just didn't realize it. I thought I wasn't good enough to be her friend. She has encouraged me a lot. We go out to lunch when we both have the time. But she likes me for who I am. I went to her and told her I wanted to write a book to help other people who are going through what I went through because there just aren't enough self- help books out there to read and she encouraged me to write this and she has been my co-pilot through all of this.

I'm not in a relationship at this time and I don't know if I'll ever be in one, but it is in God's hands and if it is meant to be then it will happen, and if not that's okay too. I believe everything happens for a reason so we will see. After 5 years of attending college, I received my Bachelor's Degree in Social Work in May of 2007.

I recently had an experience where I saw the behavior coming out and did it any way. I went out with a man, we played a few games of pool then went out dancing, I brought him home with me to have sex with him, knowing I really didn't want to but felt obligated because he paid for everything, (That's the compulsive disorder coming out.) I felt dirty, I knew it was wrong because I was having sex for the wrong reason and yet I couldn't seem to stop myself. But I saw all the bad behaviors coming out. It was stuff I learned in the past coming back out and I knew it. But I learned that I can't live my life in the past and that I am now able to distinguish my bad thoughts and behaviors and turn them into something more positive. I learned that a relationship is not based on sex; that it is based on honesty, trust and real love, not pretend. If there are no feelings there, then it isn't the right relationship. Now I have red flags that go up when I know things are not right and I listen to them.

There are times when I see my brothers and they treat me like crap and I just let it roll of my back because if I let what they say bother me then they win. It would show them they have power and control over me still. I'm not going to give them any more power. One thing about your abusers is that they know your self-esteem is low, so they like to try and keep it down. They don't want to see you build yourself up because once you do then they start losing control over you. As long as they can keep control, then they continue the game of making sure your self-worth is gone.

Another thing I have learned through all of this is that my abusers don't want me to be successful and the best way to get back at them is to show them differently. I have survived well. I have changed my whole life around and am succeeding in what I want to do and they don't like it because it tells them that the game is over. I WIN. They still are unhappy with their own lives and marriages and still living in their own guilt-ridden world and I pity them.

My oldest son just got married to a beautiful wonderful young women and he is a successful cop in a local police department. I think that if I didn't get healthy then my kids wouldn't either and I didn't and don't want that for my kids. I don't want my kids growing up with the same feelings of shame as I had, and that's what keeps me going. My other three kids are doing well academically. They are learning through me that they can be anything they want to be when they grow up; all they have to do is want it badly enough and they can succeed. I support them 100% as well as they support me and my choices.

Since I started this book, I have accomplished my goal of facing most of my abusers. I'm not saying everyone should do this because you don't know what the outcome will be, but since I faced two of them they have treated me with more respect as a person. Also one was able to talk to me about what he went through growing up. I was so busy going through my own abuse and I never saw what he went through. His was bad too, but it doesn't excuse him for what he did to me.

Therapy has changed to every four weeks. I feel I'm ready to go on to every four weeks, but at the same time I sometimes feel that I still need to see her before the appointment comes up because she has been my support as well as my therapist. Things have been going well for me and I have turned a few more things around in my life, such as like no longer playing the victim role, and letting go of people who bring me down .I have also read a book that helped me entitled *What Happy People Know* by Dan Baker, Ph.D. He talks about how we need to appreciate life and the things we have. Also that status and money doesn't make us happy. We have to make ourselves happy and get rid of the hate. As victims we carry around a lot of hate and it is not healthy to carry that baggage with you.

The time is going to come when I will no longer need therapy and it's suppose to be exciting, almost like graduating from a school. Which it will be, but it will also be the time to teach the world that life can get better if you believe in yourself and love yourself enough to make the right changes in your life. I will miss my therapist dearly, but there are others out there who need her more than I do. She has gone above and beyond the call of duty to help me and, if I was able to find that right therapist, then don't give up because you will too.

Conclusion

I wrote this book in hopes that everyone who has been a victim of child sexual abuse will reach out and get the help he or she needs. There is hope out there. You just need to take the first step and not give up hope. You can live a better and healthier life if you sincerely want it. I hope this book gives you the support you need to get started and helps encourage not to give up too soon. If I can do this, so can you. Just think of how it would feel to be free of the guilt and shame and live a "normal" and healthy lifestyle. I enjoy my quiet moments alone and I basically am living free of all the past. Only you can change your life around and I am here to tell you it feels great to be a survivor. I wish you success!

Book That Helped Me Heal

Albom, Mitch. *Tuesdays with Morrie.* New York: Doubleday, 1997.

Henderson, Nan, Benard, Bonnie, Sharp-Light, Nancy, ed. *Resiliency In Action.* California: Resiliency in Action, Inc., 1999.

Jampolsky, Gerald G., MD. *Love Is Letting Go of Fear.* California: Celestial Arts, 1979.

McGraw, Phillip C., PhD. *Family First.* New York: Free Press, 2004.

McGraw, Phillip C., PhD. *Self Matters.* New York: Free Press, 2001.

Pelzer, Dave. *A Child Called "It"*. Florida: Health Communications, Inc.,1993.

Pelzer, Dave. *Help Yourself.* New York: Penguin Group, 2000.

Pelzer, Dave. *The Lost Boy*. Florida: Health Communications, 1997.

Pelzer, Dave. *A Man Named Dave*. New York: Penguin Putnam, Inc., 1999.

Pelzer, Dave. *The Privilege of Youth*. New York: Penguin Group, 2004.

Urban, Hal. *Life's Greatest Lessons - 20 Things I Want My Kids to Know, 3rd edition*. California: Great Lessons Press, 2000.

About The Author

Lisa is the 9th of 14 children from a very small rural community in the Southern Tier of New York State. She is a devoted single mom of four children ranging in ages from 12 to 22. After many hard years of therapy, Lisa is happy to know her years of perseverance have helped her become whole again. At the age of 46 she completed her Bachelor's degree in Social Work, finished writing *Out of Darkness Into Light,* and is currently searching for a job that will enable her to use both her book learning and her experiential knowledge to advocate for those in need. Lisa's philosophy is to REACH FOR YOUR DREAMS - don't let things from your past become roadblocks to your success and happiness.

Printed in the United States
200647BV00003B/16-72/A